Everybody's Buddie

Everybody's Buddie

The Story of "Uncle Bud" Robinson

by

Ruby Robinson Wise

ILLUSTRATED BY CELIA JOLLEY
GREAT-GRANDDAUGHTER OF BUD ROBINSON

BEACON HILL PRESS OF KANSAS CITY
Kansas City, Missouri

ISBN: 0-8341-0460-1

10 9 8 7

Bud Robinson *loved* big crowds—
for this reason
it seems very fitting to me
that a story about him
should be dedicated to
his 14 grandchildren,
32 great-grandchildren,
and
13 great-great-grandchildren
who "serve this present day"
from the pulpit and the classroom;
through art, music, medicine,
the written and spoken word,
industry, and commerce;

with affection and admiration,

—Ruby Robinson Wise

History in a Tennessee Cabin

There was a foot of new snow outside the little, windowless Tennessee cabin. The wind, blowing through the trees, made blustery noises. Presently, inside the cabin, there was a small wail.

The neighbor women looked at Martha and smiled. "You have a son," they said.

Martha's smile was tired, but she answered promptly, "His name is Reuben." The neighbor women bathed the baby, wrapped him warmly, and tucked him into the cradle by the fireplace. The date was January 27, 1860.

The cabin had one room, a big fireplace, a bed built into the corner, a table, a spinning wheel and small loom. The furniture was rather crudely made. The cradle was simply a hollowed-out log mounted on rockers. There were quilts and a few sheepskins stacked in a corner. These were spread out at night by the fire for the children to sleep on.

The morning after the baby was born, the children, who had stayed overnight with a neighbor, were told

They all crowded around the log cradle to look at the baby

about the new little brother. So right after breakfast they "lit out" for home. Jake and Amanda, who were 18 and 16, looked after the little ones—Belle was 7, Andy 6, Owen 4, and Sallie 2.

When they reached home, they all crowded around the log cradle to look at the baby. They were told that he was named Reuben; but looking at him, they decided that he was their "little Buddie," and the name stuck.

The cabin was in a small valley, surrounded by beautiful wooded mountains. There was enough flat land for a cornfield and pasture. There was a spring with a hollowed-out log for a water trough, the overflow running down to a nearby creek. As primitive as the cabin was, it was as good as the homes of most of the neighbors.

Emanuel Robinson had brought his bride here. Her name was Martha Jane Adkins. She was the only daughter of the tavern keeper at the crossroads. She had been married before and had one daughter, Margaret. When her husband was killed in a hunting accident, Martha came home to live with her parents.

Emanuel was possibly 20 years older than Martha. His first wife had died, leaving him with a son, Jake, and a daughter, Amanda. Emanuel persuaded the young Martha to marry him and move to the log cabin. He claimed that he was paying "the highest taxes in the county." Maybe he was. But before too long the various kinds of "bad luck" that can dog the tracks of a maker of "moonshine" began to be felt in the Robinson cabin. The older sons helped with the farming, often without the help of the father, who frequently had to leave the family to elude the "revenuers."

In this family group Buddie grew from an infant in the hollow log cradle to the "little Buddie" who tagged along after the other children.

Early Memories

When Buddie got older, there were two clear memories from his very early childhood that remained with him. The Civil War was almost over. One day a small group of Union soldiers came through the valley. They were "requisitioning" needed horses. The Robinsons had an old horse affectionately called "Old Gin." When a soldier dismounted and went over to the stable, Martha barred his way. He pushed her aside and went into the barn. But Martha followed, snatched up a bridle, and began beating the soldier over the head with it. There followed a noisy scuffle: The children were crying, the soldier swearing, Martha continuing her blows with the bridle as she expressed her opinion of horse-stealing Yankees.

Eventually the soldier succeeded in taking the bridle away from her and putting it on Old Gin. He mounted his own horse and rode out of the yard with Old Gin in tow. Martha called after him, "You'd better get a good ride today, because this is the last day you will ever ride Old Gin; for if God spares my life, I will have old Pleas Parr and the Texas guerrillas on your track before night."

The soldiers went about 12 miles farther, came to a small community and secured more horses. They were eating supper when old Pleas Parr and his men came across the mountains. They fought under a black flag, and it was said they never gave or took prisoners.

There was quite a skirmish. As the Union soldiers rode for cover, most of them were picked off by the guerrillas. By the time they had reached the Robinson farm, most of the soldiers had been killed. As they neared the house, Old Gin left the road, tried to jump a ditch, and fell. The soldier riding her jumped clear and ran off through the field.

Martha and Jake climbed into the ditch, got hold of

When a soldier dismounted and went over to the stable,
Martha barred his way.

the bridle reins, and with much pulling, lifting, shoving, and encouraging, got Old Gin on her feet. She was soon out of the ditch and headed toward home. They bandaged a cut on her leg, using all the home remedies they knew. In a week, Old Gin was able to work again.

The second memory was much happier. As he recalled later, Buddie was quite sure he was about four years old. The children were playing in the yard. Their mother had gone from the cabin through the cornfield to the spring to get a bucket of water. Martha had stopped to pray by the spring; and as she prayed, she had been wonderfully blessed.

She started back to the cabin, shouting "Glory!" as she came. She looked so radiantly happy that Buddie, small as he was, desperately wanted to feel like that. He went out into the apple orchard and prayed, but nothing happened. Possibly he did not tell anyone how he felt—and maybe his mother thought he was too young to understand about prayer. At least no one helped him. But he never forgot how happy his mother had looked.

Fun and Games

The cabin was in a beautiful valley. Beyond the cornfield, apple orchard, and pasture was a creek and beyond that the woods. With so small a cabin and so many children, most of the playing was done out of doors. The older boys hunted and fished. The children also hunted, using the bows and arrows they had made, and fished with string and bent pins.

In the spring they looked for wild berries. In the fall, they found nuts. Sometimes they brought armloads of corncobs from the barn and made their own toy fences and pigpens. One day it was Buddie's turn to be the "pig" and his brother, Andy's, turn to be the hunter.

Andy, at 10, was a much better shot than any of them expected—and Buddie wore a scar behind his ear for the rest of his life.

One day the children decided to go to the woods to play "wild horses." They would first find a small, slender tree, bend it over until someone could climb on its end, then turn loose. The rider would have quite an exciting experience!

The children did not attend any of the occasional revivals that were held in the community. But they had heard neighbors describe the shouting—especially when "Aunt Duese" had been baptized. So they invented a new game called "The Baptizin'."

One hot morning when they were tired of their "wild horse" riding, they decided to go on down to the creek, cool off, and play "Baptizin'." They found a convenient chunk of wood to be "Aunt Duese." Owen and Andy were to throw Aunt Duese into the creek after Buddie had preached a bit, then Belle and Sallie were to shout. The game was going well when it was interrupted.

Martha, up in the cabin weaving, heard the screaming down by the creek and thought someone had drowned. She came running through the cornfield, terrified at what she might find. When she discovered that she had interruped a "baptizin'," she just spanked everybody!

On winter evenings, if the big boys had been lucky in their hunting, there would be baked possum, sweet potatoes roasted in the hot ashes, and corn bread or biscuits. The children played guessing games or counting games while the food cooked.

The Trip to Mississippi

With so many happy experiences shared by a devoted mother and many brothers and sisters, it is strange that Buddie remembered his childhood as sad and hard. He was afraid of his father, who was tall and strong. For those times, he was considered educated and once owned much property.

Buddie's earliest memory of him was his storming into the cabin one night, taking the gun down from over the fireplace, and announcing angrily that he was on his way to kill a certain neighbor. Another neighbor came in; and in the scuffle which followed, the neighbor succeeded in taking the gun away from Emanuel. The children cowered in a corner, terrified by this stormy scene.

Emanuel's temper was easily triggered and he was very profane in his speech. It is no wonder that Buddie and perhaps the older children too would run and hide when they heard their father coming.

As Buddie got older, he resented more and more his father's abuse of his mother. Not much was said to explain his father's frequent absences. The family was aware of the raids the revenuers were making. And everyone knew of Emanuel's moonshine stills and that he sold liquor in the general store that he owned and operated.

In 1865, when Buddie was five years old, Emanuel decided to try to better his condition by moving to Mississippi. Some household items were sold, the rest were loaded into a covered wagon, and the long trip was started. They arrived in Tippah County just before Christmas and settled near the little Tallahatchie River. The fishing and hunting was good here. Soon, however, the horses died of something called "the blind staggers." Now there was no way to cultivate the land. Next Emanuel rented a farm on "shares." The landlord was to furnish a team. After the crop had been planted, there was a quarrel and the landlord took the team. That left Emanuel with no means of cultivating and harvesting the crop. So the crop was lost.

Then they tried to make a living in the tar business. The children collected pine knots, kilns were built, the knots burned, and the dripping tar was collected. The work was hard and dirty and the profits very meager. So Emanuel decided to turn to a business he knew well. He rented a still and began making whiskey.

As often happened, he had trouble with the owner of the still and an almost-fatal fight followed. This seemed to convince Emanuel that Mississippi was no place for him, so in the fall of 1869 the family returned to Tennessee. Buddie was just nine years old.

The trip took 21 days. The wagon was pulled by two oxen, "Nig" and "Jerry." These were tiring days to Martha, who carried an infant and looked after the small children. They were happy days for the older children who walked beside or behind the wagon, looked for nuts and berries, fished and hunted.

They traveled until they found the same old cabin in the same beautiful valley. Martha and the children were delighted to be back home again. Emanuel hated to see the old neighbors, afraid that they would look down on the family for having failed.

15

A New Friend

When Buddie was about 10, it became his regular chore to go to the mill. The shelled corn was put in bags and laid over the horse's back—then Buddie got on and rode bareback or up on top of the corn. The water mill where the corn was ground was several miles away. Here customers had to wait their turns, which gave boys a lot of time to play.

Soon Buddie became friends with another boy about his own age, and the usual mountain invitation was given: "Come over to my house and stay all night."

When Martha realized how much Buddie wanted to go, she gave her consent. This meant walking miles over the "pig trails" through the mountains to his friend's home.

Buddie arrived in the late afternoon and was greatly impressed by the house. It was large, built of hewn logs. There was a rock chimney and a wood floor. The fireplace had a big stone hearth. There were featherbeds around the walls. There was a separate kitchen with a second fireplace. Here was a long table with a white tablecloth and dishes which he always remembered. When they were seated and quiet, the father asked a blessing, then began serving the plates. His food looked so good that Buddie almost wanted to save it—but not quite.

After supper the family moved into the other room. Buddie noticed that the parents talked to each other and smiled while the children played games. Then apples were brought up from the cellar. When they had finished eating them, the children sat down with their feet toward the fire and listened while the father read a chapter from

The shelled corn was put in bags and laid over the horse's back. Then Buddie got on and rode bareback or on top of the corn.

the Bible and prayed for each one, not forgetting Buddie. The prayer was that God would save him and make him a blessing to his family and to the world.

As Buddie walked back over the mountains the next day, he had much to think about—the big house, the good food, the big table and white cloth, the kind father and mother, and the prayer. He resolved then that when he was a man he would be like that father, and his house would be the same kind of house.

The Death of Emanuel

In 1872, when Buddie was 12, Emanuel made a trip to Missouri. This was where several relatives lived, including his first wife's people. While visiting there, he received the news of the birth of a baby girl. He wrote back naming the baby Mary Katheryn. She became "Mollie" almost as promptly as Reuben had become "Buddie."

Emanuel was making plans to return to Tennessee when he became fatally ill. When he realized that he could not live, he was deeply troubled about the way he had lived. He felt that everything was very dark, and he was afraid to go out into the darkness. He asked to have someone come and pray with him. Before he died, he told the relatives that the darkness was gone—now everything was light and he was not afraid. This was the most comforting word that Martha could have received.

The family continued to live on the same farm for the next four years. These were years of growing anxiety for Martha. She saw the pattern of drinking and fighting in the community. She was troubled about the lack of a school or church. She finally decided to sell everything and move the family to Texas. By this time Jake, Amanda, and Margaret were married. Martha and the other 10 children traveled by wagon to Nashville, then by train to Dallas, Texas. They found a place to live in nearby Lancaster. The older boys found jobs on neighboring farms, and Buddie began working on a cattle ranch.

The Circuit Rider

As Buddie worked on the ranch, he began to adopt the looks and manners of a cowboy. Of course he had

18

a wide-brimmed hat, boots and spurs, and a six-shooter. He also began to take part in the usual pastimes in the bunkhouse. The ranch owner and his wife gave dances from time to time. They also owned a racehorse. These things seemed fun to Buddie, but he was never even tempted to drink along with the other cowhands. Even so his mother was troubled about him and began praying more earnestly for him.

One evening, when the chores were about done, a horse was heard in the distance. As he came nearer, the rider was heard singing. This was rather surprising. When he rode up to the gate and greeted everyone, he announced that he was a Methodist circuit rider, and he had come to spend the night.

He dismounted and asked Buddie to feed and water his horse and put him up for the night. As he walked into the ranch house, decks of cards began to slide into hip pockets, and conversation became noticeably mild. When supper was ready, before anybody could start spearing meat or grabbing biscuits, the circuit rider said, "Hold on here, young men. We're going to ask a blessing." Everything became as still as death.

When the meal was over and chairs were being pushed back from the table, the preacher again stopped them. "Young men," he said, "don't leave until we have had family prayers." And no one left!

He opened his saddlebag, took out a Bible, and read a long chapter about heaven. Then he prayed, telling God how badly these men needed forgiveness, how wicked they were and how hopeless. He ended by praying, "Great God, keep these men out of hell tonight." Things were really quiet in the bunkhouse that night, but there was restless turning in bed.

At breakfast the next morning the preacher again asked a blessing and again read and prayed when the meal was over. Then his horse was brought from the barn, and he was ready to go on his way. Before he mounted, he shook hands all around and said, "My friends, I can't get back to see you for a month." No one had asked him back, but everyone stood around and watched him ride away, singing as he went.

Sure enough, about a month later the singing horseman was heard again. This time everyone was down to the gate to meet him. After shaking hands, he announced, "I am going to stay with you two or three days this trip." The men all wondered how they could live through it.

Camp Meeting

As the circuit rider was leaving this time, he told everyone about a camp meeting he was planning to hold in August. The place, about 20 miles from the ranch, was called the Old Bluff Springs Campground. A rich rancher had been converted and offered to give all the beef the campers could use.

Martha heard of this camp meeting. She had an invitation to go with a neighboring family, and she insisted that Buddie go too. When they arrived, they found that there were covered wagons and tents all around the camp meeting shed. The women cooked the donated beef, made biscuits and coffee, and everyone ate together at a long, outdoor table.

Buddie had really gone to have a vacation and fun, with no intention of "seeking religion." But one evening something happened to change all this. The minister had asked all the Christians to "find a sinner and pray with him." An elderly woman with white hair (Buddie thought she was almost 100 years old!) came to the back row and spotted Buddie. Before he knew what was happening, she got down in front of him, put her hands on his knees, and started to pray. Buddie wanted to leave, but he felt like he was glued to the bench. She prayed louder and louder and finally began to shout as though she knew her prayer was going to be answered. She got up and left without saying a word to Buddie. He finally left the shed and walked around the campground, feeling more miserable all the time.

That evening Buddie noticed that a different man was going to preach. The first preacher had been tall. He wore a long coat and had a long beard. The preacher who stood this evening was shorter, his beard was also short, and he wore a short coat. Buddie looked at him and thought, "I bet that man can't preach a lick. He is going to be a failure." But as the man began to picture Christ coming to earth and dying on a cross, he made it all seem so real that Buddie felt like it had happened just last week, somewhere in Texas.

When the people were invited to come to the altar for prayer, many went forward. Buddie wanted to go too, but really did not know how to start or what to do. Then an elderly preacher with long, white hair came down the aisle and said, "Is there a young man back here who wants to meet me in heaven? Come, give me your hand." Buddie was saying to himself, "I can do that much." By the time he reached the old preacher, he was crying.

The preacher took him by the arm and started him down the aisle to the split-log mourner's bench. After much prayer the burden of sin was lifted. When Buddie stood to his feet, he thought everybody looked like angels! He was the one who was changed, however.

His Call to Preach

When the service was finally over, Buddie went to the place where he had been sleeping. On the way he threw his deck of cards into someone's campfire and tossed his revolver into the ravine. He knew he wasn't going to need them any longer. He put his hat over a mesquite stump for a pillow and lay looking at the stars. He felt like God had brought them all out on parade for him. Before he went to sleep, he was sure that Jesus spoke to him and asked him to preach. Without any hesitation, he promised that he would.

The next morning after breakfast, he heard singing, so he followed the other campers to the big shelter (a "brush arbor" they called it) where somebody said there was to be a "testimony meeting." As Buddie listened to various people tell about their conversions, he became more and more excited. Finally he noticed one of the big posts that supported the arbor. It seemed like a good idea to express his feelings by climbing to the top of it—so up he went!

This was almost like a signal for general shouting. There followed a time of rejoicing, of witnessing, and of confessing. Everyone was talking of the goodness of God.

When the group finally became quiet, the preacher

He was sure that Jesus spoke to him and asked him to preach. Without any hesitation, he promised that he would.

said, "We are going to open the doors of the church." This really puzzled Buddie. There was no church for miles. The arbor had no doors. But when everyone began to sing "Amazing Grace" and a number of people started moving to the front, Buddie decided to go along. When it was his turn to shake hands with the preacher, he was asked, "My son, what church do you want to join?"

Buddie answered, "I don't know. How many have you got?"

The preacher listed Baptists, Presbyterians, Christians, Methodists. Buddie said, "Which one are you in?" He answered, "Methodist." So Buddie said, "Put me in that one."

But the next puzzle had to do with "How do you want to be baptized?" Buddie answered, "I don't know. What do you do to a feller when you baptize him?" So the various methods of baptism were described. The one that seemed just right to Buddie was "pouring"; so when he had knelt down and had repeated the church vows, water was poured from a small pitcher onto his head. He said much later when telling of this experience: "That preacher had baptized boys with more sense than I had, but he never baptized one that shouted louder or enjoyed it more."

Starting to Preach

When the camp meeting was over, Buddie quit his job on the ranch and moved back home. He got a job with a neighboring farmer digging stumps for 50 cents a day. About three months later when the family learned of a Sunday school in the community, they began to attend.

The Sunday school teacher gave Buddie a small New Testament, and he began the difficult task of trying to read it. Reading called for writing, so he began to copy verses from Matthew on the barn door, saying to himself, "I'm going to make a man out of you, Bud Robinson, or die in the attempt!"

Whenever he was called on to pray at Sunday school or church, he began to be troubled about his "call to preach." Finally he went to see an older man in the church who said, "Don't ever try to preach. You would disgrace the cause." When Buddie promised that he would not try, the old gentleman felt much better, but Buddie felt much worse!

Then a new preacher came to that circuit. One day Buddie started to tell him about his problem, but began to cry instead. The preacher said, "Brother Bud, I know what your trouble is. God has called you to preach and you think you can't do it." Buddie nodded. The preacher promised to recommend him to the Quarterly Conference for a license to "exhort." Buddie felt like a mountain had been rolled off his shoulders.

About two weeks later the Quarterly Conference met, and Buddie went for an examination. The minister who questioned him was a very kind person, but Buddie could not answer any of his questions, which ranged from history to grammar to church discipline. He waited in another room for about an hour; and when he was called back in, he was told that the exhorter's license had been granted him.

Years later he learned what had taken place. The committee had voted against giving him a license but an older man asked them to reconsider. He said, "Brethren, we have done wrong in turning down this boy. If God has called him to preach and we stand in his way, he may backslide, and in the judgment God will require his blood at our hands. I move that we grant a license to this boy." So he was passed.

Buddie's job made it possible for him to save a little money, so one day he saddled his horse and rode about 16 miles to a small town to buy his "preacher's clothes." He bought six yards of checked cotton cloth for a coat and pants. This cost 75 cents. Then he bought three yards of speckled calico for a shirt for 15 cents. He got a straw hat for 25 cents and brogan shoes for $1.50. So with his outlay of $2.65 he was ready to return home and let Martha get started on the sewing.

There were no invitations to preach; but when the new clothes were finished, Buddie began a routine of finding a schoolhouse where he could preach. Then, on Saturdays, he would ride from ranch to ranch, telling everyone that there would be preaching in the schoolhouse the next day.

These announcements were usually met with a great deal of amusement because Buddie stuttered badly. By the time he had finished telling where the meeting would be held, most of the ranch hands would be roaring with laughter. But they would assure him, "We'll be there." And they kept their word.

Early Ministry

When he was given his exhorter's license, Buddie had been instructed to keep a record of the sermons he preached, the prayer meetings he held, the homes he prayed in, and the number of people converted. His first report showed that in the three months, he had preached 50 times, had held 27 prayer meetings, had prayed in 95 homes, and 60 people had been converted. When he stood to give his report, he began to cry, so the presiding elder read it for him. When he finished, he said, "Brother Bud, this is a good report. The Lord is with you. Keep on preaching." And Buddie did.

For the next eight or nine years Buddie continued to preach on Sunday, farm during the week, and hold revivals after the crops were "laid by." He began paying on a farm of his own, but not much of the payments came from his ministry. He was paid about $4.00 a year for the first four years.

One time during the very early days of his ministry, he had gone out to a rather remote schoolhouse. After the Saturday evening service he was invited to go home with a family for the night. Buddie was taken to his room, and he went to bed and to sleep. In the night he was awakened by a touch. He opened his eyes and was sure an angel stood beside him, telling him to get up and pray. The angel went over and stood in the doorway. Buddie could hear voices raised in argument in another part of the house.

Presently the talking stopped. Buddie went back to bed and to sleep with the angel still on guard. In the morning when he left his room, the house seemed to be deserted. Eventually the rancher's wife came in. She looked troubled and said something about "all the menfolks had to leave." Buddie mounted his pony and rode back to the schoolhouse.

Someone asked him, "Brother Bud, where did you

stay last night?" When Buddie gave them the name of the ranch, everyone looked shocked and troubled. They explained that in the past several years travelers had mysteriously disappeared from that ranch. God's angel had protected Buddie from a similar fate.

Double Trouble

After Buddie was converted at the camp meeting, there was nothing but joy and peace for about three months. Then one morning he woke up feeling awful: blue, depressed, discouraged. He began to wonder if he had "slept off" his religion. He tried to pray and felt that God was not listening to him. So he saddled his horse and rode over to the home of one of the church board members to tell him that he had lost his religion.

"Well, how in the world did you lose it?" the man asked.

"I slept it off in the night."

His next question was "Have you been praying?"

"Yes, but the Lord quit hearing me today, and I don't know what to do about it" was Buddie's answer.

"Well, Brother Bud, you are having your doubts now."

"What on earth are they? I didn't know a religious fellow had anything like that."

So the man explained, "When you were converted, you didn't get the old man took out, and he's in there giving you trouble. He will stay till you die; but if you live faithful 'til death, the Lord will give you a crown of life."

So Buddie returned to the farm, and after a long

season of prayer behind the barn, everything seemed right again.

On a farm, as in every other place, there are all kinds of opportunities for things to go wrong. When the mules ran away, Buddie's temper did too. When they balked, it was even worse. After each of these outbursts the devil would slip up and say, "What are you going to preach about tomorrow?" Then there would be more prayer times behind the barn. When he shared his troubles with other Christians, they seemed to think this was all perfectly normal. One of the favorite prayer meeting songs was:

Prone to wander, Lord, I feel it,
Prone to leave the God I love.

Another was:

I saw a way-worn traveler
In tattered garments clad,
And struggling up the mountain
It seemed that he was sad.

Most of the testimonies related to the ups and downs of the Christian life.

To Buddie, all the outer hardships of arduous work, few places to preach, the open ridicule of his stuttering, and his poor health were nothing compared to the inner turmoil he was having because of the "old man."

The Cure

In the year 1886, a very unique man named Dr. W. B. Godbey came to hold a meeting in a nearby town. He was a Greek and Hebrew scholar, but his sermons were preached in very down-to-earth English that could be understood by anybody. People said he was "sanctified," and everyone wondered what that meant. One of his main topics was hell, and he was very clear in pointing out the various roads to this destination. He described the people on these roads. He announced that there was no such thing as a "sinning religion." If you were sinning, you were "on the road to hell."

The first time Buddie heard him, he decided that the man was crazy and would be in the asylum before the month's meeting was over. But the longer he listened, the more logical it all seemed. Many people were converted or sanctified in that meeting, but Buddie continued his struggle against the sinful nature within.

The next year Rev. Ben Gassaway came to be the pastor. He continued the same theme that had been preached by Dr. Godbey: Christians do not have to live with continual struggles with the "old man." As Buddie listened to these sermons, he became convinced of the truth and began definitely seeking to be sanctified—to be delivered from this inner warfare. He began preaching about the promise and the possibility of being sanctified. He would explain to his congregation that he did not yet have this experience, but that he was seeking it.

Finally one day in June, 1890, he was out in the field thinning corn and preaching to himself when he came to the point of complete surrender. He felt that the Lord had come in and was taking out of his heart things that he did not even know were there. Then came a "river of peace" flowing over him.

Later he was to record that in the first year after he was sanctified, he had more people converted than in the 10 preceding years of preaching. He said it was because so much of his praying had had to be done for himself.

He was out in the field thinning corn when he came to the point of complete surrender.

Off to School

It is really hard to get a very clear picture of Buddie's schooling. One of the reasons Martha had moved her family from the mountains was because there was no school there. Martha herself was a great reader, but books were scarce and surely time, for her, was even more scarce. When Buddie received his first New Testament, he was evidently able to read only the easiest portions. But he applied himself to the task until he had taught himself to read. Soon after his sanctification his pastor urged him to leave the farm and go to school.

So, when he was 31, he entered South-Western University at the beginning of the fall term. Fortunately for him the institution had both a grade school and high school besides the college. Buddie was placed in the third grade. Here he stayed until April, when he decided he must go back to full-time preaching. Those had not been idle months, however. He had access to a library and was fascinated by the wealth he found in books. Here began his lifetime devotion to reading. He also attended daily chapel services and had the privilege of listening to outstanding church leaders of the South. He used the school situation for his parish and began very soon to have converts among the children and young people. Many of the ministerial students he led into the experience of holiness.

The Holiness Band

When Buddie received the blessing of entire sanctification that June day in the cornfield, his world was completely changed. He was positive everyone would seek this experience as soon as he heard of it. He was therefore surprised when one of his church friends said to him, "Brother Bud, you had better go slow on this thing." People who had been very friendly in the past now passed him with a brief nod. When he went to Georgetown to attend South-Western University, he found that other believers in holiness were facing the same kind of rejection. So, to strengthen one another, they organized a prayer group which they called the "Holiness Band." The friendships formed in this small group lasted throughout Buddie's life.

One of these band members was Miss Sallie Harper. Her family had lived near Georgetown since her parents had moved from Missouri before the Civil War. Her father was a doctor and a local preacher in the Methodist church. Her brothers, nephews, and nieces were well known in the community, and they found it embarrassing that Miss Sallie had joined this small, unpopular group. Not long after they met, Buddie decided that Miss Sallie was just the person he wanted for a wife. Miss Sallie did not find this decision easy; but, after much prayer, she decided to say yes with this condition: "Lord," she prayed, "if we have children, I ask for them to have good health."

They were married on January 10, 1893. They moved into a house she owned, and Buddie continued to preach wherever he could.

When there were not enough preaching opportunities to provide food for the family, Buddie took whatever work he could find, sometimes cutting wood. Once he ran a dye shop for a while, and Miss Sallie rented part of the house to students who boarded there.

"Little Sallie"

In September, 1895, a little girl was born. Buddie said she should be named for her mother, so she was christened Sallie Harper Robinson. Miss Sallie, of course, really needed someone to help her and to look after the baby, so she located Martha Eddleman. Martha was a former slave who had worked for the family in the past. She had been trained as a nurse in the household of her former owner. Her husband, Jeff, was a blacksmith. Martha was glad to come and help out. She knew that the pay would be very small, but she had a special reason for wanting to come. She had heard a little of the message of the holiness preachers, and she was hungry for this to happen to her.

Between her nursing, cooking, and housekeeping duties, she found time to talk to Miss Sallie about her heart hunger, and to tell her how much she longed for spiritual victory. She stayed on with the family for a number of years, whether they could pay her or not. Sometimes "Uncle Jeff" would stop by to leave groceries he had bought for them when times were extra hard.

Healing

Buddie always thought than an accident he had on the ranch had caused the beginning of epileptic seizures. These increased in severity until finally he reached the stage where his arms would be wrenched from the sockets at the shoulder. When the seizure was over, his brothers or the ranch hands would pull his arms back into place. The pain was severe, but the depression that followed these attacks was worse. As time passed, the ligaments became so stretched that the arms slipped out of place frequently, so he quit trying to have someone reset them. His arm movements were limited, but there was no pain.

There were other health problems, as well as the constant embarrassment of his stuttering. Finally the Holiness Band decided that the Bible definitely taught that people could be healed. Miss Sallie wrote letters to Rev. D. L. Moody and Rev. A. B. Simpson and asked them to unite their prayers with the prayers of the local group. On a certain day there was fasting and prayer and Buddie was healed. He lived to be 82, but from 1896 to 1942 there were only two or three light seizures. His general health was never really good. His stuttering never entirely disappeared but was usually thought of as lisping rather than stuttering. The memory lapses that often followed the seizures disappeared, and he became known as a person with a phenomenal memory. He used this to great advantage in memorizing scripture and in recalling names, faces, dates, places, and incidents.

The Waco Camp

After a while another baby came to the Robinson family. When this second little girl was born in 1898, Buddie announced, "She is to be named for me." So she was christened "Reuben." For a short time the two little girls were nicknamed Grace and Glory, but eventually the family roll call was simplified to: Buddie, Miss Sallie, Little Sallie, and Ruby.

The following year the family decided to make the effort to attend Waco Camp. This camp meeting was becoming very well known through the South. It was located five or six miles from the thriving town of Waco. The large tabernacle was surrounded by an area of scattered trees. There was plenty of room for campers and an area for stock. The Robinsons were able to pitch their tent near the tabernacle, close behind the platform. This made it possible for Miss Sallie to rock the baby and listen to the sermons too.

One of the evangelists was Dr. H. C. Morrison from Louisville, Kentucky. After he had met Buddie, he insisted that the camp meeting board should ask him to preach at one service. This service was greatly blessed. It was really a turning point in Buddie's life. He knew this was just exactly what he wanted to do. The friendship of these and other holiness preachers was the beginning of a great brotherhood reaching into many denominations.

The Hubbard Circuit

After the family returned home from the Waco Camp, Buddie asked for, and was given, a "circuit." This meant that he was responsible for pastoring several churches. The family moved to Hill County where Buddie was to organize the Hubbard Circuit. This was a pattern that he was used to: riding from place to place, asking for the use of schoolhouses for services, praying in the homes of the people. But it was not a particularly happy experience. The parsonage was very primitive. There was much illness in the family. Both Miss Sallie and little Ruby had the recurring chills and fever common to that area. The financial support was also very poor. But possibly more irksome than anything else to Buddie was the routine that did not seem to be accomplishing anything. During those months on the Hubbard Circuit Buddie saw clearly that his work was to be as an evangelist, not a pastor.

In 1899 he was called to hold a revival meeting in Greenville, Texas. While he was there, he learned of plans to start a holiness school in a nearby small community named Peniel, and he decided to move his family there. In August of 1900 he resigned as pastor of the Hubbard Circuit and moved to Peniel.

Peniel

Peniel was a small village built, for the most part, like a hollow square with a large brick building, the first unit of the school, in the center. There was a general store on the east side and another store and the post office on the west. The families who settled here could buy a single lot, or more if they desired. Buddie and Miss Sallie invested the money from the sale of the house in Georgetown, and bought enough land to have a yard, a peach orchard, and a small pasture. While the house was being built, the family rented rooms from the school's first president, Dr. A. M. Hills.

For a family of four, the house was unbelievably large: five rooms on each of the first and second floors and four attic rooms above that gave ample room. But Buddie and Sallie were almost never alone. Usually several students stayed with them. Soon after the house was completed, the students began moving in. A varying

For a family of four the house was unbelievably large, but
Buddie and Sallie were almost never alone.

number of boys roomed on the third floor. Several girls and the family occupied the second floor. The house was heated by four fireplaces in the downstairs rooms, a big black stove in the kitchen, and small wood-burning stoves in the bedrooms.

The house had porches across the front on the first and second floors and one across the back on the first floor. Just behind the kitchen was the cistern. A rope, a pulley, and a big bucket brought up the water. A very small room was closed in at the west end of the back porch to be a playhouse for Sallie and Ruby. Here shelves with partitions housed the doll families.

The livestock consisted of cows, horses, and chickens. The barn loft was usually about half full of cotton seed hulls. This made a wonderful place to play. The students who lived with them took care of the place, the boys looking after the stock and chickens, the girls helping with the housework. Laundry was done in the backyard where the white clothes were boiled in a big iron pot. Clothes lines were nearby in the side yard.

This was a wonderful place for children to grow up. As Sallie got a bit bigger, she showed a remarkable talent for music. Sometimes one or another of the students would be the teacher. Later she studied at the school. When Ruby got past a passionate devotion to her dolls, Buddie bought her a horse and a sidesaddle, and there were a few riding lessons. Later there were art lessons.

Church in Peniel

In the very beginnings of the school and the village, the camp meeting was the center of interest. Land had been donated, a wooden tabernacle built, and plenty of wooded land set off to accommodate campers. When the village site was surveyed, it occupied the area south and west of the campground. After the central brick building was completed, wooden buildings followed.

The people involved in these early beginnings were from various church backgrounds. Their common bond had grown from the holiness bands. The services were conducted by faculty members. There was no village activity apart from church or school activities. Everyone went to everything.

The Larger "Circuit"

Buddie's preaching was an itinerant ministry. In the early years, the distances were covered on horseback. This was true also on the Hubbard Circuit, and the trip to the Waco Camp Meeting was by covered wagon. But things began to change. The requests to hold meetings came from farther away.

Thus began the period of his life when he "lived in a suitcase." Two railroads came through Greenville (two or three miles from Peniel), so there was ready access to any part of the country. By 1902 he had begun traveling with Rev. Will Huff. Miss Sallie went with them for about a year and a half, leaving the two little girls in the care of a grown-up cousin, Margaret Price.

While on one of these trips an incident happened that Miss Sallie always remembered. The trip was by chair car and the train was crowded, so that they could not sit together. Buddie, fast asleep, was sitting where Miss Sallie could see him. Presently a man came in and stood at the end of the car, carefully looking over the passengers. His dress and manner marked him as a gambler, a "city slicker" or a card shark. He seemed to have selected Buddie as an easy mark. He went over, woke him, and asked if he could change a $20.00 bill.

Buddie slowly opened his eyes, looked at the stranger, and asked, "Brother, is it good money?" The stranger was profuse in assuring him that the bill was good. Buddie answered, "Mine is too. I can't see why you should wake a fellow up in the dead of night just to swap good money," and promptly went back to sleep.

In 1906, while preaching in Los Angeles, Buddie learned that Dr. Bresee was interested in visiting the South, so he was invited to come to Peniel. There on April 6, he organized the independent group of worshipers into a new congregation of the Church of the Nazarene.

In 1907 the Church of the Nazarene on the west coast and a group of holiness churches of the east coast met in Chicago. The two groups joined and called the new denomination "Pentecostal Church of the Nazarene." In 1908 the southern holiness people joined this group at Pilot Point, Texas. All of this brought about a greatly enlarged opportunity for Buddie to travel. He usually came home for a few days every few months, but sometimes these visits did not add up to more than 10 days during the year.

During the years in Peniel, before the group joined the Church of the Nazarene, a publishing house had been formed and a weekly paper called the *Texas Holiness Advocate* was published and distributed to the members of the various holiness bands. Buddie was a stockholder in this company and contributed articles to it regularly. He also began writing occasionally to other holiness periodicals.

After the merger of the southern group, the *Texas Holiness Advocate* was discontinued and the holdings of the publishing house were turned over; and a new paper, the *Herald of Holiness,* was launched in 1912 to serve the whole denomination. This became one of Buddie's hobbies. He would say, "I have two themes: holiness and the *Herald of Holiness.*"

He was a very enthusiastic worker for new subscriptions, which he always called "subs." His meetings were increasingly with his own denomination, but he was just as enthusiastic about getting "subs" in a union revival as anywhere else. He once said, "If a feller didn't have the dollar to subscribe, I *guess* it would be all right for him to steal the dollar, because by the time he had read the first copy he would have got under conviction, got saved, paid back the dollar, and then he would have the other 51 copies!"

Buddie's friends liked to tell about taking him to the zoo. Of course Buddie had a copy of the *Herald of Holiness* in his pocket. He was standing, leaning against the cage housing the monkeys, when a hairy arm reached through the bars and grabbed the *Herald.* The monkey retreated up a tree, where he sat turning the paper this way and that. The other men said, "Buddie is not content to just get the Nazarenes to read the *Herald,* he has started on the monkeys now!"

As the years passed, a pattern of district tours was developed. This would be at the request of the district superintendent. On these trips often a third emphasis was added to holiness and the *Herald of Holiness*—that of home missions.

Pasadena

In June of 1912 the family moved to Pasadena, California. Much thought had gone into this change. Miss Sallie had been feeling the severe and sudden "cold spells" of the Texas winters. Buddie had thoroughly enjoyed his contacts on the west coast. About this time, by a happy turn of events, the Smee family decided to move to Peniel and wanted to buy the house, the acreage, and the stock owned by the Robinsons. A boxcar on a siding was loaded with the household goods of the Robinsons and the Merritt Hills, who were also moving to Pasadena. A lot was found near the college there, and the construction of a new house begun. In the meantime, the family stayed in the boys' dormitory on the campus. The garage was finished by the time school began, so the family "camped" here until the house could be occupied about Thanksgiving.

Buddie's traveling continued, sometimes alone, sometimes with an evangelistic party. Always he loved it. For nearly 30 years he crisscrossed the country, and the name of "Uncle Bud" Robinson became a household word.

In 1913 Little Sallie at 17 married Rev. W. A. Welch, whom she had met in Peniel. They moved to Whittier where he pastored the Church of the Nazarene. Ruby was still in the grade school department of Pasadena College. But the house was not empty. There were always students in the home as there had been in Peniel.

The Accident

The year 1919 was very busy. Buddie was to hold a revival in San Francisco with Rev. C. E. Cornell, in connection with the district assembly. One night on the way back to his hotel from the church, he was starting to cross the street when he saw a car coming very fast. He jumped to avoid it, but this put him in the path of an oncoming streetcar. Jumping again, he landed in the path of another car which struck him. The impact hurled him 30 feet. The police were called and he was taken to the emergency hospital.

Not until 1:30 a.m. did the authorities succeed in reaching Rev. Cornell. He, with Rev. Donald Smith and Rev. Shelby Corlett, came to the emergency hospital and arranged for Buddie to be moved to the Leland Stanford Hospital. Rev. Cornell sent telegrams to the family. The examination showed that both arms were broken; the left leg was broken, the knee shattered, and the ankle fractured. The necessary surgery was performed on June 3. There followed weeks of convalescence. At one time when he thought he could not bear the pain, there was special prayer at the church and the pain was relieved.

Eventually the doctors decided that he could be moved back to the Los Angeles area where he would be near home. He was taken by stretcher to the train, loaded into a Pullman car through a window, and removed from the train the same way. He was taken to the Huntington Memorial Hospital and finally was released to go home. Even though he had to see the doctor every day, he was finally told, "Brother Bud, you would be better off preaching." So, still having difficulty with his arm and walking with a cane, he took the train for Boston.

Jumping again, he landed in the path of another car which struck him.

Dreams

Buddie was really a down-to-earth person, but three visions in his life had great significance for him. The first was the "angel's visit," which he told to only a few close friends. The other two have been recounted in his books. One of these two had a great bearing on his feeling of urgency about preaching and happened early in his ministry.

In his dream he was standing beside a rushing, muddy stream. Many people were struggling in the water and he was wading out, snatching as many as he could and bringing them to shore. From that time on the phrase "lost souls" always reminded him of that vivid dream.

The second dream came to him when he was in the hospital, soon after his accident. This was a very vivid dream of going to heaven. The people and places were very clear to him, and the music was beautiful beyond description. He said that he really wanted to stay, but God sent him back to finish the work he was to do.

From the time of the accident, Buddie continued to travel, following his usual pattern of spending a few days at home followed by many months away. There were changes at home now, however. Sallie and Rev. Welch had moved to a ranch near Richgrove, California. Ruby had married Rev. George C. Wise. Since the church they pastored was nearby, and since "Miss Sallie" was not strong the Wises continued to live in the family home. Buddie was extremely proud of the grandchildren, remembering their birthdays and telling everyone that there "wasn't a scrub in the bunch."

The Holy Land

In February, 1934, a dream came true for him. He was a member of a party of friends who made a tour of the Holy Land. Since he had a remarkable acquaintance with his Bible, he was thrilled when he could now see "where it all happened." He probably prayed and quoted scripture at every stop, and certainly reveled in all the facts and figures the guide gave him. He was most grateful for the kindness of Rev. S. Krikorian, pastor of the church in Jerusalem.

Family Changes

The Wises moved from the Pasadena home in 1939. Rev. Wise had been called to pastor the Church of the Nazarene in Glendale. "Miss Sallie" missed the grandchildren very much, but would not let her feelings interrupt this call to service. Different friends stayed with her from time to time, so that her routine remained much the same. She was a woman of prayer, faith, hospitality, loyalty, and devotion.

In her early eighties she survived an attack of appendicitis. Buddie had come home because of her illness. But on September 29, 1940, she slipped away at sunrise, having been ill with pneumonia.

The next two years were very difficult for Buddie. In 1941, now past 80, he developed heart trouble. The Wises returned to Pasadena in 1942 where they were better able to take care of him.

In January of that year Buddie decided to really celebrate his 82nd birthday. His strength was limited but he would walk a few blocks each day. On these trips he would chat with neighbors and friends and invite them all to come to his birthday dinner. Presently the family began to suspect that no one really knew just who or how many had been invited. Relatives and friends helped with the preparation of the food, tables were borrowed from Bresee Church, and, on the evening of January 27, 1942, 74 of his friends and relatives sat down to dinner with him. This made him supremely happy.

During the spring and summer his activity was limited. He enjoyed having old friends come to see him.

When he became bedfast, his moods varied. Sometimes he was troubled over "having done so little." Sometimes he was confused and felt sure he was waiting for a train to get to the next meeting. And sometimes he was sure that "heaven can't be far away."

And really, it was not. He died on the evening of November 2, 1942.

Many wonderful things were said about him at the memorial service. Possibly the greatest tribute was demonstrated by the long line of people of all ages and all classes who came to pay him this final honor.

Members of the family (children, grandchildren, and great-grandchildren) continue to be grateful that Buddie is remembered with love by so many people. He still is "everybody's Buddie."

www.ingramcontent.com/pod-product-compliance
Lightning Source LLC
Chambersburg PA
CBHW060542030426
42337CB00021B/4397